I SPY

WITH MY LITTLE EYE

CHRISTMAS

LET'S PLAY

I SPY

MEZZO
ZENTANGLE
DESIGNS

I SPY WITH MY LITTLE EYE SOMETHING BEGINNING WITH...

A IS FOR

ANGEL

I SPY WITH MY LITTLE EYE SOMETHING BEGINNING WITH...

B IS FOR

BELL

I SPY WITH MY LITTLE EYE SOMETHING BEGINNING WITH...

C IS FOR CANDY CANE

I SPY WITH MY LITTLE EYE SOMETHING BEGINNING WITH...

 IS FOR

 WITH MY LITTLE EYE SOMETHING BEGINNING WITH...

 IS FOR

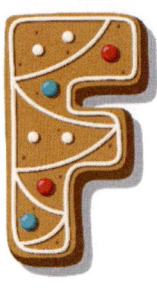

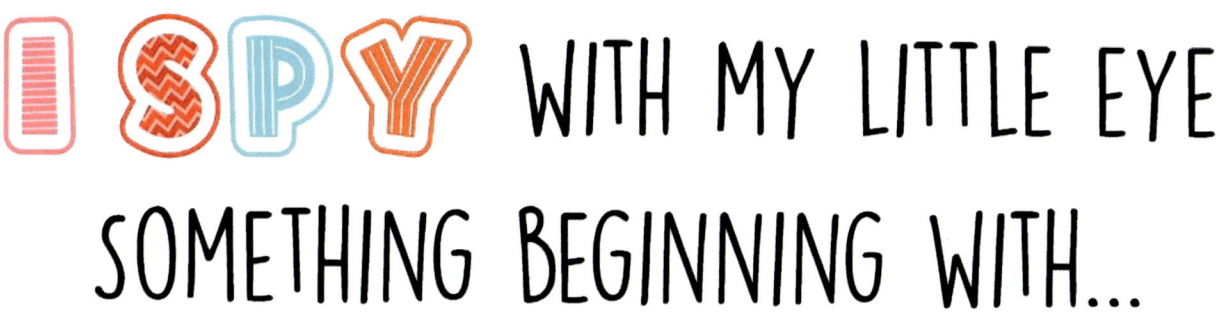

I SPY WITH MY LITTLE EYE SOMETHING BEGINNING WITH...

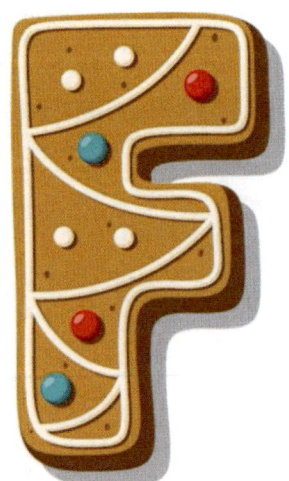 IS FOR

I SPY WITH MY LITTLE EYE SOMETHING BEGINNING WITH...

G IS FOR GIFT

I SPY WITH MY LITTLE EYE SOMETHING BEGINNING WITH...

G IS FOR

GINGERBREAD

I SPY WITH MY LITTLE EYE SOMETHING BEGINNING WITH...

H IS FOR

HOLLY

I SPY WITH MY LITTLE EYE SOMETHING BEGINNING WITH...

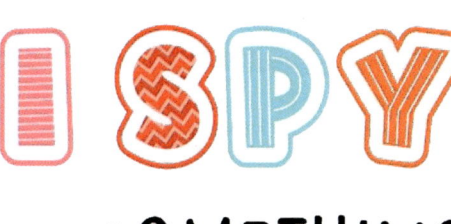

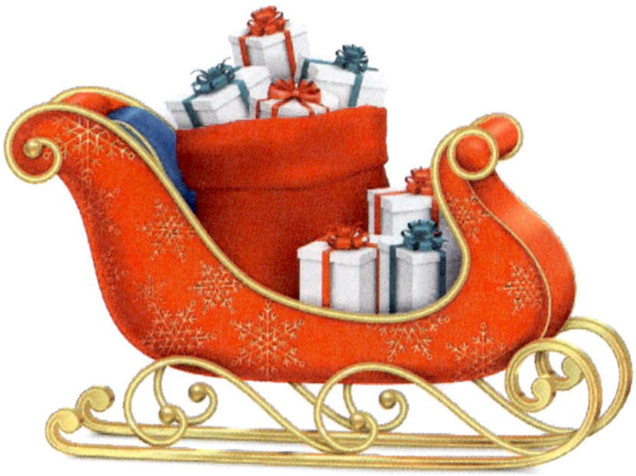

L

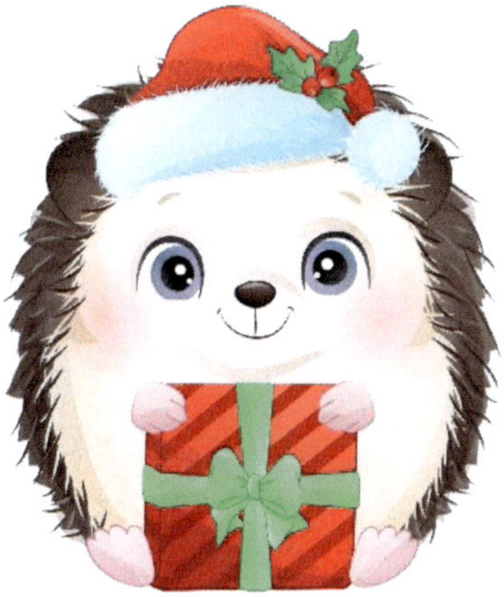

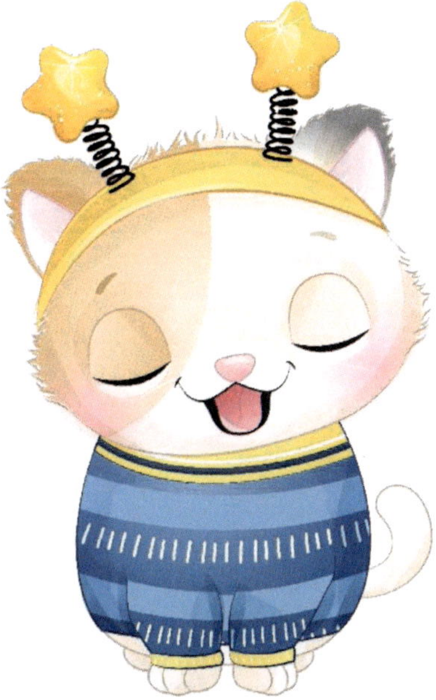

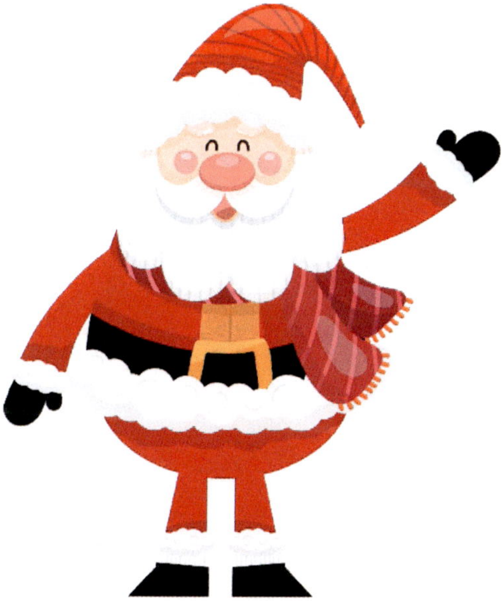

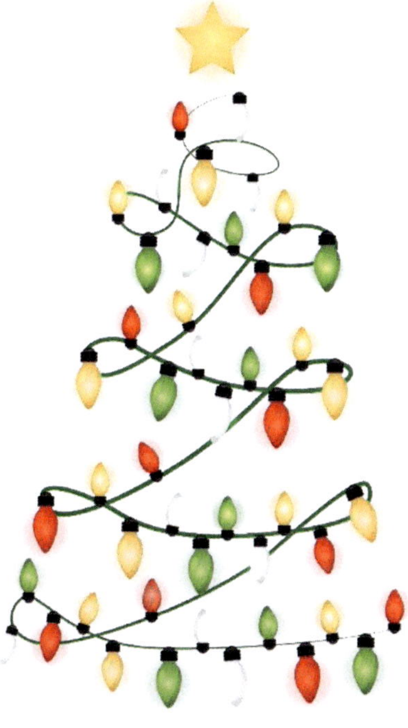

L IS FOR LIGHTS

I SPY WITH MY LITTLE EYE SOMETHING BEGINNING WITH...

 IS FOR

I SPY WITH MY LITTLE EYE

SOMETHING BEGINNING WITH...

O IS FOR

ORNAMENTS

I SPY WITH MY LITTLE EYE
SOMETHING BEGINNING WITH...

P IS FOR PUDDING

 I SPY WITH MY LITTLE EYE

SOMETHING BEGINNING WITH...

R

R IS FOR REINDEER

I SPY  WITH MY LITTLE EYE SOMETHING BEGINNING WITH...

 **IS FOR**

I SPY WITH MY LITTLE EYE SOMETHING BEGINNING WITH...

S IS FOR

SLEIGH

I SPY WITH MY LITTLE EYE SOMETHING BEGINNING WITH...

S IS FOR SNOWMAN

I SPY WITH MY LITTLE EYE SOMETHING BEGINNING WITH...

S IS FOR STOCKING

I SPY WITH MY LITTLE EYE
SOMETHING BEGINNING WITH...

T IS FOR

TOYS

I SPY WITH MY LITTLE EYE

SOMETHING BEGINNING WITH...

T IS FOR

TREE

I SPY WITH MY LITTLE EYE

SOMETHING BEGINNING WITH...

W IS FOR

WREATH